HISTORY OF
THE CHESAPEAKE BAY

By Therese Shea

Gareth Stevens
Publishing

Please visit our website, www.garethstevens.com. For a free color catalog of all our high-quality books, call toll free 1-800-542-2595 or fax 1-877-542-2596.

Library of Congress Cataloging-in-Publication Data

Shea, Therese.
History of the Chesapeake Bay / by Therese Shea.
   p. cm. — (Exploring the Chesapeake Bay)
Includes index.
ISBN 978-1-4339-9773-0 (pbk.)
ISBN 978-1-4339-9774-7 (6-pack)
ISBN 978-1-4339-9772-3 (library binding)
1. Chesapeake Bay (Md. and Va.)—Juvenile literature. 2. Chesapeake Bay Region (Md. and Va.)—History—Juvenile literature. I. Shea, Therese. II. Title.
F187.C5 S24 2014
975.2—d23

First Edition

Published in 2014 by
Gareth Stevens Publishing
111 East 14th Street, Suite 349
New York, NY 10003

Designer: Andrea Davison-Bartolotta
Editor: Kristen Rajczak

Photo credits: Cover, p. 1 courtesy of the US Navy; p. 4 (map) © iStockphoto.com/crossroadscreative; pp. 4–5 (background), 28 iStockphoto/Thinkstock; p. 5 (main) Stocktrek Images/Thinkstock; p. 7 courtesy of NASA; p. 8 AbleStock.com/Thinkstock; p. 9 Photos.com/Thinkstock; p. 10 Dea Picture Library/Getty Images; p. 11 Stock Montage/Getty Images; pp. 12, 13 Hulton Archive/Getty Images; pp. 14–15 DEA/M. Seemuller/Getty Images; p. 16 Steve Heap/Shutterstock.com; p. 17 The British Library/Robana via Getty Images; pp. 18, 25 Cameron Davidson/Photographer's Choice/Getty Images; p. 19 (top) courtesy of Wikimedia Commons; p. 19 (bottom) Kean Collection/Getty Images; p. 20 (inset) MPI/Getty Images; pp. 20–21 (main), 23 courtesy of the Library of Congress; p. 22 Buyenlarge/Getty Images; pp. 24, 29 Greg Pease/Photographer's Choice/Getty Images; p. 27 Globe Turner/Shutterstock.com;

Printed in the United States of America

CPSIA compliance information: Batch #CS13GS: For further information contact Gareth Stevens, New York, New York at 1-800-542-2595.

CONTENTS

Words in the glossary appear in **bold** type the
first time they are used in the text.

THE ARM OF THE ATLANTIC

The Chesapeake Bay is a large inlet of the Atlantic Ocean. It looks like an arm reaching into the eastern coast of the United States. This "arm" is around 200 miles (322 km) long and ranges from about 4 to 40 miles (6 to 64 km) wide. Ships enter the bay off the coast of Virginia and continue north through Maryland. The Chesapeake cuts Maryland in half.

Many rivers empty into the Chesapeake Bay, making it an estuary. An estuary is a partly enclosed coastal body of water in which the freshwater of rivers and the salt water of oceans mix freely.

MARYLAND

DC

VIRGINIA

NEW JERSEY

DELAWARE BAY

DELAWARE

MARYLAND

CHESAPEAKE BAY

CHESAPEAKE BAY

POTOMAC RIVER

ATLANTIC OCEAN

OTHER ESTUARIES

Now that you know what an estuary is, think of some other bodies of water that may be estuaries. San Francisco Bay and the mouth of the Mississippi River are two more American estuaries. Estuaries have always been important to people because they're **hubs** of transportation as well as sources of seafood.

Many rivers empty into the bay, including the Susquehanna, the James, the York, the Rappahannock, and the Potomac Rivers.

A LONG, LONG TIME AGO...

The Chesapeake Bay was millions of years in the making. Geologists think a comet or asteroid landed about 35 million years ago near what is now Cape Charles, Virginia, which is where the bay opens up to the Atlantic. The crater made from the impact was as wide as Rhode Island and as deep as the Grand Canyon!

During the last **ice age**, thick glaciers spread as far south as present-day Pennsylvania. When these glaciers began to melt about 18,000 years ago, the water made its way to the ocean, carving into the land over thousands of years. This led to the beginning of the bay's formation 12,000 years ago. About 3,000 years ago, the Chesapeake Bay began to look much like it does today.

A VERY LOW TIDE

When the Chesapeake Bay was first forming, sea levels were much lower than they are now. In fact, the Atlantic coast was about 180 miles (290 km) farther east than it is today. As the glaciers melted, the waters rose, filling in the valley that had been carved by waters and raising sea levels.

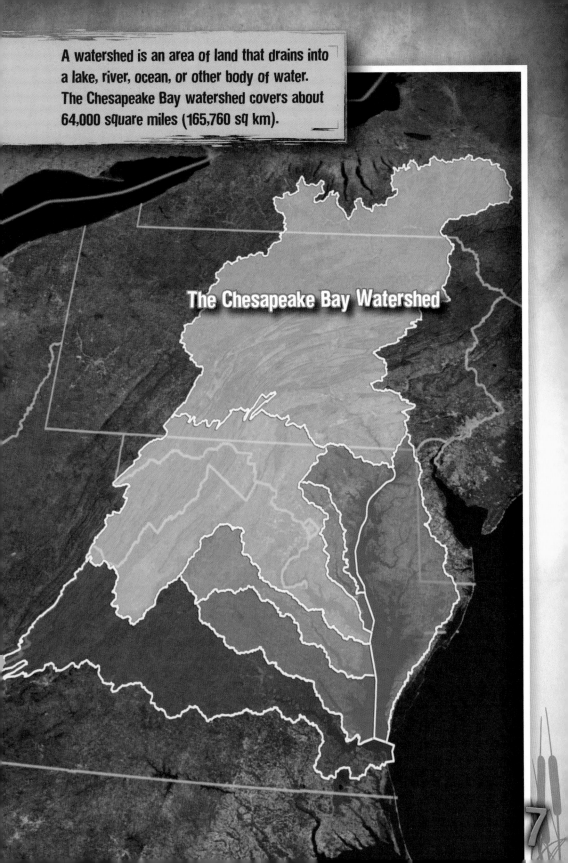

A watershed is an area of land that drains into a lake, river, ocean, or other body of water. The Chesapeake Bay watershed covers about 64,000 square miles (165,760 sq km).

The Chesapeake Bay Watershed

WHO WAS FIRST?

There's a lot of confusion about the first European explorer of the Chesapeake. No records of the famous early explorers offer proof that they were the first. However, one account from 1570 tells of a Spanish ship that sailed into the Chesapeake Bay. It went up the James River and stopped near present-day Newport News, Virginia. The Spanish built the Ajacán (ah-hah-KAHN) **mission** on the York River. However, Native Americans killed most of the settlers.

Native Americans had been living on the bay for thousands of years before these or any other Europeans showed up. And many, many more Europeans would arrive, beginning with the Jamestown settlers.

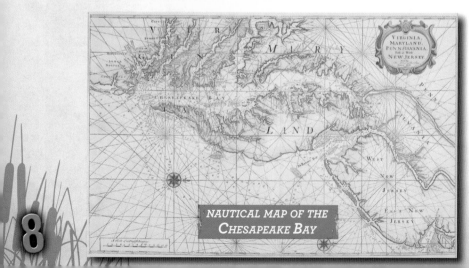

NAUTICAL MAP OF THE
CHESAPEAKE BAY

NATIVE AMERICANS OF THE CHESAPEAKE

The Chesapeake Bay's name comes from the Algonquian Indian word *chesepiooc* which some say means "great shellfish bay." It may also mean "people on the great river." Around 1600, the area was home to perhaps 13,500 Powhatans, a tribe of Woodland Indians. As in other parts of North America, the European arrival meant the death or removal of many of the native peoples.

England first made claims in Virginia in 1584. In 1632, the British king granted Maryland to Lord Baltimore. Little thought was given to the native peoples who already lived there.

JAMESTOWN'S FIRST YEARS

Jamestown was the first permanent British colony in America. A group of more than 100 men landed in Virginia in April 1607. They began building a colony on the James River in May.

Captain John Smith, a member of the governing council, helped keep the colony going its first years despite **famine**, disease, and native attacks. He worked to establish trade with the nearby Powhatans, so the settlers had food until they could grow enough of their own. But the harsh winter of 1609, called the "starving time," left only 60 settlers alive. The survivors nearly left, but supplies arrived from England just in time.

JOHN SMITH'S MAP OF THE CHESAPEAKE BAY (1612)

JOHN SMITH, EXPLORER

John Smith explored the Chesapeake Bay twice in 1608. He had several goals: mapping the area, finding riches, trading with Indians, and discovering a route to the Pacific Ocean. He made it to the head of the bay, the Susquehanna River. At one point, Smith was stung by a poisonous fish, but he recovered and ate it for dinner! In 1609, he returned to England.

Though John Smith never returned to America, his maps and writings provided valuable information for future settlers and historians.

THE GROWTH OF CHESAPEAKE SETTLEMENTS

Settlers of the Chesapeake region were attracted to the same resources: easy water routes into America and back out to the Atlantic, an abundance of land and water for farming, plentiful wildlife for hunting, and an accessible fishing industry.

George Calvert—Lord Baltimore and a Roman Catholic—wanted to create a place in America that tolerated all religious beliefs. He was granted the land that became Maryland by King James I, a Protestant. Calvert died in 1632 and passed the land to his son, Cecil. In 1633, Cecil's brother led a group of colonists up the Potomac River. In 1634, they founded Saint Mary's City, Maryland's first city and capital.

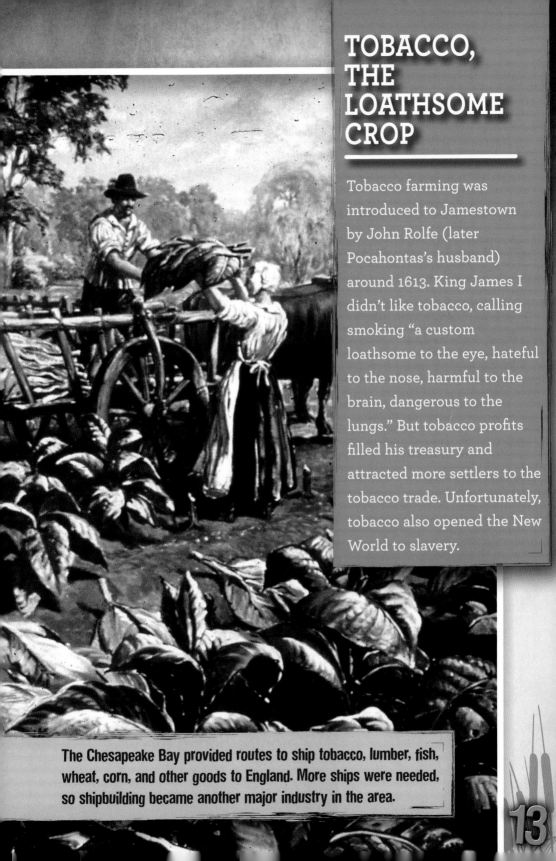

TOBACCO, THE LOATHSOME CROP

Tobacco farming was introduced to Jamestown by John Rolfe (later Pocahontas's husband) around 1613. King James I didn't like tobacco, calling smoking "a custom loathsome to the eye, hateful to the nose, harmful to the brain, dangerous to the lungs." But tobacco profits filled his treasury and attracted more settlers to the tobacco trade. Unfortunately, tobacco also opened the New World to slavery.

The Chesapeake Bay provided routes to ship tobacco, lumber, fish, wheat, corn, and other goods to England. More ships were needed, so shipbuilding became another major industry in the area.

Baltimore, Maryland, was founded in 1729 as Baltimore Town, though its port began operating years earlier in 1706. The town was meant to be a center of Maryland's growing tobacco trade, but wheat and flour were Baltimore's most profitable exports by the late 1700s.

THE BATTLE OF THE CHESAPEAKE

In 1781, British general Cornwallis and his troops arrived in Yorktown, Virginia, to await ships to take them to New York City. America's French **allies** sent naval ships to the Chesapeake Bay to stop the British from leaving. The British and French navies met at the Battle of the Chesapeake. Neither side truly won, but the British navy was forced to leave Cornwallis and his men behind.

England's Navigation Acts made it illegal to ship certain goods, including tobacco, anywhere but England. This was a way for the British government to control prices, collect taxes, and keep profits. Colonists soon wanted more say in trade. The Navigation Acts and similar laws led to the **American Revolution**. Baltimore was the new nation's capital for about 2 months during the war.

The Battle of the Chesapeake led to the **Siege** of Yorktown, where 8,000 British troops surrendered. This didn't win the American Revolution, but made British officials begin to consider peace talks. The war lasted until 1783.

PIRATES OF THE CHESAPEAKE

With so many goods and money traveling in and out of the Chesapeake Bay, some people saw a way to get rich quick—pirating! Pirates waited for ships to pass along the coast and plundered their goods.

Lionel Wafer, John Hinson, and Edward Davis were three pirates who stole riches near South America. After deciding to retire to Hampton Roads, Virginia, they traveled a land route from Delaware Bay to the northern Chesapeake. They began to sail south but were captured in 1688. The men were later set free because they gave part of their loot for the founding of the College of William and Mary.

This statue of a Virginia governor stands in front of the library at the College of William and Mary.

HELPFUL PIRATES?

Some pirates acted under orders. Merchants, colonial officials, and others sometimes hired them to capture ships. Several laws kept colonists from receiving goods from certain countries, but pirates followed their own laws! The city of Baltimore was called a "nest of pirates" because ships from Baltimore did such great damage to British vessels.

The famous pirate Blackbeard, whose real name was Edward Teach, captured a ship off Cape Charles, Virginia, in 1717. He then retired to North Carolina—but his head was brought back to Virginia following a **duel**!

THE CHESAPEAKE IN WARTIME

During the War of 1812, enemy British naval forces headed into the Chesapeake Bay, knowing that it was a center of trade and government. The British navy **blockaded** ports in Maryland and Virginia, and reached Washington, DC, on the Potomac River on August 24, 1814. Soldiers burned the Capitol, White House, and many other buildings.

Next, the British sailed up the Patapsco River to Baltimore. The naval force attacked Fort McHenry in Baltimore Harbor, but not even 25 hours of cannon and gunfire could make the fort surrender. The ships withdrew. British land forces also couldn't overcome Baltimore's defenses, and soon Americans took control of the Chesapeake again.

FORT McHENRY

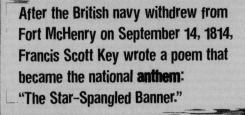

After the British navy withdrew from Fort McHenry on September 14, 1814, Francis Scott Key wrote a poem that became the national **anthem**: "The Star-Spangled Banner."

THE *CHESAPEAKE* VS. THE *LEOPARD*

In 1807, off the coast of Norfolk, Virginia, the British ship *Leopard* asked to board the American ship *Chesapeake* to search for British deserters. The captain of the *Chesapeake* refused. The *Leopard* fired on the Americans and boarded the ship. British deserters were found, and American sailors were **sentenced** for protecting them (though never punished). US citizens were outraged, and the incident was one of the causes of the War of 1812.

In the years leading up to the **American Civil War**, the Chesapeake Bay region was divided over slavery. While the states of Maryland and Delaware remained in the Union, Virginia joined the Confederacy in 1861.

Union and Confederate forces were ever present in the Chesapeake and often used the bay for the shipment of supplies and troops. In 1862, a huge Union force sailed to the Confederate capital of Richmond, Virginia, on the James River. However, the troops were forced back to Washington, DC. By 1864, a Union fleet called the Potomac **Flotilla** had driven most Confederate forces out of the Chesapeake Bay.

THE UNDERGROUND RAILROAD

Between 1830 and 1860, the Chesapeake Bay and its connecting rivers were a major part of the Underground Railroad, a network of paths and people who helped slaves escape to the North. Harriet Tubman was born into slavery on Maryland's coast. She escaped and returned to the South 19 times to lead more than 300 slaves along the Underground Railroad to freedom.

HARRIET TUBMAN

In March 1862, **ironclad** warships called the *Virginia* (or *Merrimac*) and the *Monitor* fought near Hampton Roads. The battle had no clear winner, but the Union's *Monitor* prevented the Confederacy's *Virginia* from destroying the ships at the Hampton Roads port.

THE BOOMING BAY

After the Civil War, freed slaves flocked to the bay to find jobs. Many were employed by the seafood industry, specifically harvesting oysters. By the 1880s, the Chesapeake Bay was a world leader in oyster production.

Railroads, such as the Chesapeake & Ohio, had solidified the Chesapeake region as a center of both land and sea transportation. Coal mined in West Virginia was some of the most important cargo.

GIANT CRANE IN USE AT
NEWPORT NEWS SHIPBUILDING

It was sent by train to Newport News, Virginia, and then shipped by boat across the country and beyond. New shipyards were built to create more vessels for shipping. Newport News Shipbuilding employed 12,000 people by 1920.

The "Oyster Wars" were sometimes-violent conflicts involving oyster fishermen (also called watermen), both legal and illegal, in the Chesapeake Bay during the 1800s and early 1900s. There was even an oyster navy to police waters!

THE CHESAPEAKE-DELAWARE CANAL

Besides railroads, another transportation route was constructed off the Chesapeake Bay in the early 1800s: the Chesapeake-Delaware Canal. The water route connects the bay to the Delaware River, allowing ships to skip the nearly 300-mile (483 km) trip around the coast of Maryland and Delaware and opening up the North Atlantic trade route. The canal first opened in 1829 and is still used today.

23

TODAY'S CHESAPEAKE

Shipbuilding never ceased being a major part of the Chesapeake economy. Today, Newport News Shipbuilding is the sole designer, builder, and refueler for US aircraft carriers and one of two providers of US Navy submarines. Nearby Norfolk, Virginia, is the world's largest base for the US Navy. Portsmouth, Virginia, has one of the world's largest shipyards for repairs.

Hampton Roads and Baltimore, Maryland, continue to be two of the East Coast's busiest ports, transporting manufactured goods, coal, tobacco, and agricultural products. Agriculture is still a big part of the Virginia economy—especially chicken. And Maryland's reputation for seafood is only matched by its status as a center of technology and research.

THE CHESAPEAKE BAY BRIDGE-TUNNEL

In 1964, an incredible achievement of engineering was completed—the Chesapeake Bay Bridge-Tunnel. Just over 17 miles (27 km) long, it connects southeastern Virginia (Norfolk and Hampton Roads) to Cape Charles on the Delmarva **peninsula**, also known as the Eastern Shore. The road is supported by 5,000 piers. A tunnel allows for cars to pass under the bay while ships pass over.

The Chesapeake Bay Bridge connects the eastern and western shores of Maryland. Before this bridge and the Chesapeake Bay Bridge-Tunnel, people had to take boats from one shore to the other or drive long distances.

MAPPING CHESAPEAKE HISTORY

Use the key to find out where many important events in the history of the Chesapeake Bay happened.

Key

- Newport News (first European landing in 1570)
- Jamestown (founded 1607)
- Saint Mary's City (founded 1634)
- Battle of the Chesapeake (1781)
- Yorktown (siege in 1781)
- Washington, DC (burned 1814)
- Battle of Baltimore (1814)
- Chesapeake-Delaware Canal (opened 1829)
- Richmond (named Confederate capital, 1861)
- Battle of Hampton Roads (1862)
- Chesapeake Bay Bridge (opened 1952)
- Chesapeake Bay Bridge-Tunnel (opened 1964)

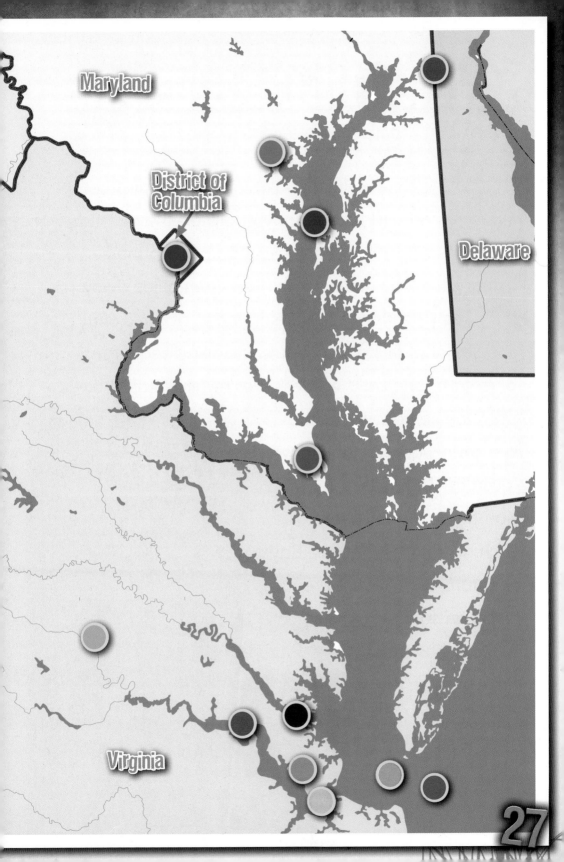

Maryland

District of
Columbia

Delaware

Virginia

27

SAVING THE CHESAPEAKE

The price of the Chesapeake's success is high. Overfishing and pollution have taken their toll. The industries around the bay have polluted the air and water. And because many rivers empty into the estuary, the bay receives pollution from miles away.

The Chesapeake Bay is home to about 3,600 species of plants and animals, including sea turtles, blue crab, and bald eagles. They're all affected by pollution somehow. People are even warned about how much fish they can safely eat! Many organizations, such as the Chesapeake Bay Program, work hard to reduce pollution so the bay has a future as rich as its past.

SAVE THE OYSTERS!

One of the benefits of a wild oyster population is that they filter and clean water. Shockingly, Maryland's current oyster population is less than 1 percent of what it was in the early 1800s. In order to help wild populations grow, areas have been protected to help the oysters bounce back, but it will take time.

Tourism is another major industry of the Chesapeake Bay. People are fighting to keep its waters and coasts beautiful for visitors for years to come!

GLOSSARY

ally: one of two or more people or groups who work together

American Civil War: a war fought from 1861 to 1865 in the United States between the Union (the Northern states) and the Confederacy (the Southern states)

American Revolution: the war in which the colonies won their freedom from England

anthem: a song declaring loyalty to a group, cause, or country

blockade: to block passage to ports with ships

duel: formal combat with weapons fought between two people in front of witnesses

famine: a shortage of food that causes people to go hungry

flotilla: a large number of ships sailing together

hub: a place that is a center of activity

ice age: a period during which temperatures fall worldwide and large areas are covered with glaciers

ironclad: covered with iron or steel for protection

mission: a place where church leaders teach their beliefs and help the community

peninsula: a narrow piece of land that sticks out from the mainland into a sea or lake

sentence: to name a punishment for a crime

siege: blocking off a fort or city with soldiers so that nothing can get in or go out

FOR MORE INFORMATION

Books

Bennett, Kelly. *Chesapeake Bay*. New York, NY: Children's Press, 2006.

Mis, Melody S. *The Colony of Maryland: A Primary Source History*. New York, NY: PowerKids Press, 2007.

St. Antoine, Sara, ed. *The South Atlantic Coast and Piedmont: Stories from Where We Live*. Minneapolis, MN: Milkweed Editions, 2006.

Websites

Chesapeake Bay: An Estuary in Crisis
www.marinersmuseum.org/sites/micro/chesapeake_bay/index.php
Find out more about the problems facing the Chesapeake Bay and possible solutions.

Chesapeake Bay Program
www.chesapeakebay.net/history
Read about important events in the bay's history.

INDEX